OUP

Prayers of Jesus

HEARING HIS HEARTBEAT

CWR

Peter Hicks

Published 2011 by CWR, Waverley Abbey House, Waverley Lane, Farnham, Surrey GU9 8EP, UK. Registered Charity No. 294387. Registered Limited Company No. 1990308.

See back of book for list of National Distributors.

Unless otherwise indicated, all Scripture references are from the Holy Bible: New International Version (NIV), copyright © 1973, 1978, 1984 by the International Bible Society.

Concept development, editing, design and production by CWR

Cover image: istock/Yury Kuzmin and istock/aaM Photography, Ltd.

Printed in England by Page Bros.

ISBN: 978-1-85345-647-3

Contents

Introduction

Jesus was a man of prayer. Again and again we read of Him praying, from the moment of His baptism to His last loud cry on the cross. Luke specifically states, 'Jesus often withdrew to lonely places and prayed' (Luke 5:16). But only a tiny proportion of His prayers are recorded in the New Testament. What He prayed in those 'lonely places', or during the nights of prayer on the deserted mountainsides, we are not told.

Sometimes, perhaps, we can find something of a clue to the content of His prayer from the context in which He was praying. As He stood praying after His baptism (Luke 3:21) we can safely assume He was opening Himself to the outpouring of the Spirit and dedicating Himself to the ministry that lay ahead. As He spent the night on the mountainside before the choosing of the Twelve (Luke 6:12) we can be pretty sure He was praying over those He would be appointing. Then later, when, after the feeding of the 5,000, the people were going to make Him king by force and He went up onto a mountain alone to pray (John 6:15; Mark 6:46), we can picture Him struggling with the issue of which way forward He should follow.

Of the half dozen or so prayers of Jesus that are recorded for us in the New Testament, only one, John 17, is of any length, and even what we have there is almost certainly only a summary of a much longer prayer. But even if none of His actual prayers had been kept for us, there is so much we can learn both from the fact that prayer was so important to Him, and from the way He prayed. Jesus at prayer is our inspiring model.

Certainly He inspired His disciples. Luke describes for us a significant incident: 'One day Jesus was praying in a certain place. When he finished, one of his disciples said to him, "Lord, teach us to pray ..."' (Luke 11:1). As they watched Him at prayer they realised how inadequate their own praying was and how much they had yet to learn. It will be a key aim of this series of studies that we will not only watch Jesus at prayer, but we ourselves will learn from Him so that our own prayer lives are deepened and enriched and become more like His.

To many today the concept of learning to pray may seem a touch odd. After all, we might think, prayer is so natural we simply do it without having to learn how to do it. Indeed, most of us would feel that, in fact, we're well experienced in prayer; we've been doing it for years; we've heard thousands of prayers said by others; maybe we've even got books on it. What more do we need?

But then we look a bit more carefully. We look at great men and women of prayer, prayer warriors, heroes of faith and we feel ashamed of our own prayer life. We look into the New Testament and watch the Early Church at prayer, with the building shaken and amazing miracles in answer to prayer, and we find it rather strange. We hear of Epaphras 'always wrestling in prayer' (Col. 4:12) and we wonder what that means. We read what Paul said about his own praying, and we work through some of his recorded prayers, and we are greatly humbled. Supremely, we look at Jesus, and we know we still have a very long way to go.

So this series of studies is an opportunity to learn. Primarily, of course, it is an opportunity to learn about Jesus, to see Him more clearly as we focus on this aspect of His life and ministry. But it is also an opportunity to learn from Him, to come with the disciple's request, 'Lord, teach us to pray', and to find joy and riches as He answers that prayer.

Much of the material we will be looking at is well
known and very familiar to most of us. That's a definite
advantage; we start with a good understanding and will
be able to enrich the discussions with our mature insights.
But it's also a challenge: to ensure that we encounter the
familiar words not just as old friends but as the living and
exciting Word of God that is speaking today into our lives
and situations. So sometimes in our studies we'll approach
the material from a specific angle that will help focus
our thinking, perhaps in a fresh way. At other times we'll
simply let the well-loved words speak again their truth
and their power to our hearts. Either way, may you, and
all those you share with in these studies, find much joy,
many riches and the special blessing of the praying Jesus.

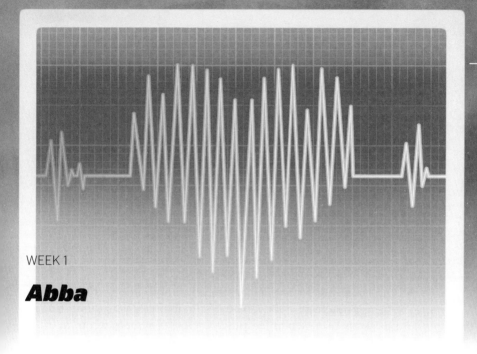

WEEK 1

Abba

Opening Icebreaker

Invite each person in the group, who is willing, to describe his or her father in one or two sentences. Then together compile two or three sentences to describe our Father God.

Bible Readings

- Mark 14:32–36
- Romans 8:12–17
- Galatians 4:4–7

Focus

Before we look at the content of Jesus' prayers, we will let the word *Abba* take us to the heart of what prayer was for Jesus.

Opening Our Eyes

In this study we're going to do something unusual. We're going to spend the whole time on one word. What's more, unlike, say, 'predestination' or 'sanctification', it's a little word, and a very simple word at that; so simple that for many children it's the very first word they learn to say.

But being small and simple and easy to learn in no way detracts from the wonder and glory of the word *Abba*. It's undoubtedly one of the most wonderful words in the whole Bible, one whose meaning and implications are so profound we would need a lifetime to experience them all.

There are four things we need to note about *Abba* as we approach this study. The first is that this was the word Jesus used when He prayed. Gospel writers wrote in Greek and so had to translate Jesus' Aramaic prayers into Greek; as a result *Abba* became *Pater* which our English translations render 'Father'. But, as Mark 14:36 shows, the word behind 'Father' in the prayers of Jesus is *Abba*. David typically started his prayers 'O LORD', or 'O God'; Solomon began, 'O LORD, God of Israel', Elijah started with 'O LORD, God of Abraham, Isaac and Israel'; Daniel began with 'O Lord, the great and awesome God'. Great ways of approaching God, all of them; but Jesus simply said '*Abba*'.

Secondly, Jesus' use of *Abba* was new and startling. The Jews, and some other contemporary religions, had a concept of God as Father in a broad and general sense, but they very rarely used it in their prayers. Jesus, by contrast, used *Abba* in the most personal and intimate way, and He used it every time He prayed. (The only 'exception' was Mark 15:34 where His prayer was in fact a quotation of Psalm 22 verse 1.)

Thirdly, the meaning of *Abba* is rich and significant. As the word little children used to address their 'daddy', it is full of simplicity, closeness and trust. But it's also more than that. In our culture we tend to stop using 'Daddy' as we grow up, feeling that it's rather childish. But Jewish children didn't stop using *Abba*; grown men and women would still use it to address their father, expressing closeness, love and respect. It spoke of a relationship as beautiful and as real and open as the child's, but now mature and enriched by understanding and experience.

Fourthly, Jesus taught His followers to use *Abba* when they prayed. Doubtless there is a place for using grander titles when we address God, but when His disciples asked Him to teach them to pray, Jesus' reply was, 'When you pray, say: "Father" ...' (Luke 11:2). For Jesus' early followers this was mind-blowing, and a glorious expression of their new relationship to Almighty God and of the presence of the Holy Spirit within them (Rom. 8:15; Gal. 4:6). We have two beautiful examples of Paul using 'Father' in his praying in Ephesians 1:17 and 3:14.

Discussion Starters

1. We all pray, and we all listen to others praying. Try writing down the titles most frequently used in addressing God in prayer. What might these titles tell us about our praying?

_____

_____

_____

_____

2. No earthly father is perfect, but we can see in some of them glimpses of what a perfect father might be like. Try describing a truly perfect earthly father, and then apply the description to our heavenly Father.

_____

_____

_____

_____

3. When I was a child I was taught to use 'Thou' and 'Thee' when addressing God in prayer 'as a sign of respect'. How does this square with Jesus' instruction to use *Abba*? How might we ensure that we retain a right reverence and respect before God while enjoying the intimacy of *Abba*?

_____

_____

_____

_____

4. We are usually very reticent to talk to others about our personal praying. If possible overcome that reticence for a few minutes and share things you have found helpful (or unhelpful) in drawing near to the heart of your heavenly Father.

_____

_____

_____
_____

5. How we pray, perhaps including the way we address God, will vary according to the context in which we are praying. Consider three settings:
(1) prayer in a church service where there is a wide mix of people present, including non-Christians;
(2) prayer in a prayer meeting or homegroup where everyone is a Christian;
(3) your own personal prayer time in the privacy of your own room.
What approaches to praying are suitable or unsuitable in each context?

_____
_____
_____
_____

6. Many Christians have had bad experiences of an earthly father, and so find it particularly difficult to approach God as _Abba_. What could we say or do to help such people? (If this describes you, you may like to tell what has been helpful to you.)

_____
_____
_____
_____

7. In closing, summarise what we can learn from _Abba_ to enrich our own relationship with God in prayer.

_____
_____
_____
_____

Personal Application

'When you pray, say, "Father ..."' (Luke 11:2) isn't just a suggestion; it's a command. God's desire and call to each of us is to have the same pattern of intimacy with Him as Jesus had. And, as Paul states in Galatians 4:6 and Romans 8:15, it is gloriously possible because God has 'sent the Spirit of his Son into our hearts'; we each have 'received the Spirit of sonship'.

How, then, is this going to affect your praying from now on? Will it mean less emphasis on asking for things and more time spent sitting at His feet? Could it be that you'll begin to develop a whole new understanding of what it means to have God as your Father? Will 'trust' and 'love' become more centre stage in your relationship with Him?

Why not write here the steps you are going to take, as you seek, through the power and presence of the Spirit of Jesus in you, to go deeper in your experience of drawing near to the God who longs for you to call Him *Abba*?

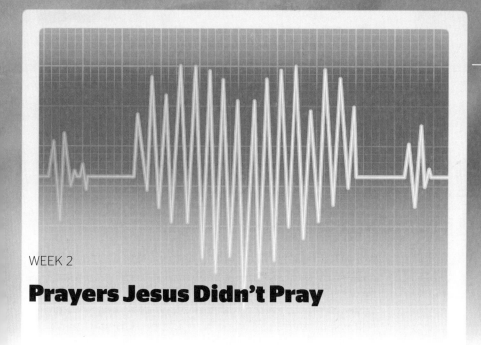

WEEK 2

Prayers Jesus Didn't Pray

Opening Icebreaker

Invite group members to share any childish 'howlers'
arising from misunderstanding of prayers or hymns, such
as: 'Our Father, which art in heaven, Harold be Thy name'
or thinking that 'God rest you merry, gentlemen' meant
that God should give them a break from being merry.

Bible Readings

- Matthew 26:47–54
- Luke 22:31–34
- John 12:23–33

- John 16:19–28
- Hebrews 5:7–10

Focus

Moving towards maturity in our praying.

Opening Our Eyes

Have you ever been tempted to assume that life is tougher for you than it was for Jesus during His time on earth? We struggle on in our very human weakness, so easily beset by sin, our vision and our relationship with God dulled and limited, and our prayer life a battle. But He had supernatural power and wisdom. His hotline to God was always open. In any situation He had all the resources of heaven at His immediate disposal. And prayer for Him, we feel, was so easy.

But if we assume that everything for Jesus was always easy we would be wrong. Life on earth for Jesus was far tougher that we can ever imagine; and, though His times of prayer were doubtless wonderful times of rich fellowship with His Father, it would be wrong to think that everything to do with prayer was easy for Him. During those long nights of prayer He would have struggled with drowsiness and wandering thoughts just as we do. The writer to the Hebrews tells us that 'during the days of Jesus' life on earth, he offered up prayers and petitions with loud cries and tears to the one who could save him from death, and he was heard because of his reverent submission' (Heb. 5:7). Some assume that the only occasion He did this was in Gethsemane, but the most natural understanding of the text is that this was a common occurrence. Like Epaphras, Jesus 'wrestled in prayer' (Col. 4:12; the Greek word used is one from which we get our word 'agony').

Further, having supernatural power and an ever-open hotline to His Father raised issues for Jesus that very few of us have to face. The devil was right, for instance, when he told Jesus that He could turn stones to bread or throw Himself safely off the highest point of the Temple (Matt. 4:3,6). But the fact that He could do these things didn't make them right. The fact that Jesus had all the resources of heaven at His disposal didn't mean that it was always right for Him to use them.

Far too many people, consciously or unconsciously, look on prayer as a kind of magic wand we can wave at any time to get us out of trouble or to make life easy. We catch a cold, so we pray for healing. We're late for the appointment, so we pray that the Lord will provide a parking space. We've not really prepared for the exam, so we pray the Lord will fix the questions. Numbers at church are dwindling, so we pray that the Lord will bring them in. And, of course, God in His grace hears and often answers such prayers. But somehow we've missed out on the 'loud cries and tears' and 'agony'.

In this study we're going to use some of the prayers Jesus chose not to pray to help us to understand a little more what true prayer is and how we should be praying. We'll start with a couple of prayers Jesus didn't pray for Himself. Then we'll consider the implications of a prayer He didn't pray for one of His followers. Then we'll look at a puzzling verse where He seems to say that He's not going to pray to God for us anymore.

Discussion Starters

1. Consider the implications of Matthew 26:53–54. Why did Jesus choose not to call on His Father? Are there times when we should choose not to do so?

_____

_____

_____

_____

2. John 12:27–28. What is happening here? What do these verses teach us about prayer?

_____

_____

_____

_____

3. 'Father, save me from this hour' is a prayer we've all prayed many times, when confronted with disaster, suffering, disappointment and the like. Does John 12:27 mean that it is wrong to pray it? What is the relationship between this prayer and the prayer in verse 28?

_____

_____

_____

_____

4. Luke 22:31–32. Jesus pointedly refrained from praying that Peter would be spared Satan's sifting. Try putting yourself in Peter's place. What might you have said if Jesus had asked, 'In the light of Satan's request, what would you like Me to pray for you?' Why do you think Jesus didn't pray for an easy time for Peter?

_____

_____

_____

_____

5. Read through John 16:19–28. What do you think is happening in this passage? Why does Jesus say in verse 26, 'I am not saying that I will ask the Father on your behalf'? Does this mean He has stopped praying for His followers altogether (see, for example, Rom. 8:34; Heb. 7:25)? How should this verse affect our praying?

_____

_____

_____

_____

6. What part might 'loud cries and tears' (Heb. 5:7) and 'wrestling in prayer' (Col. 4:12) have in our praying today?

_____

_____

_____

_____

7. If you have some spare time you might like to discuss the rights and wrongs of the prayers listed in the last but one paragraph of 'Opening Our Eyes'.

_____

_____

_____

_____

Personal Application

Here are a couple of projects you may find helpful, as you reflect on these prayers that Jesus didn't pray:

Firstly, look back over your own experiences during the past few years and recall those times when your earnest prayers did not receive the answer you hoped for. On reflection, and with the benefit of hindsight, are you happy with the way you prayed then? Can you learn anything from those experiences that will have an effect on your praying in any parallel situation in the future?

Secondly, try picturing yourself as developing into a truly mature prayer warrior. What specific steps could you be taking now to ensure that you are moving forward in that process?

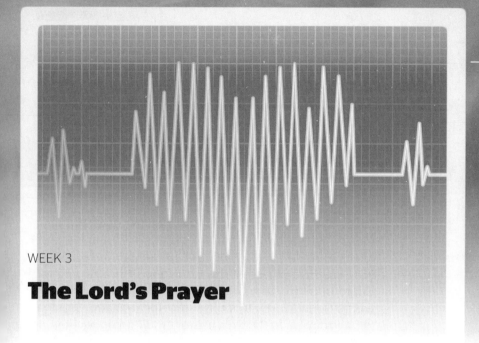

WEEK 3

The Lord's Prayer

Opening Icebreaker

Invite each member of the group to relate briefly some personal anecdote about the Lord's Prayer; for example, how they first learnt it, hearing it in a foreign language, hearing it recited at breakneck speed, and so on.

Bible Readings

- Matthew 6:9–15
- Luke 11:1–4

Focus

However familiar this prayer of Jesus may be, there are many more riches to enjoy.

Opening Our Eyes

The Lord's Prayer starts with our Father God and ends with the devil. Little wonder the Early Church soon added the familiar doxology: 'For yours is the kingdom and the power and the glory for ever. Amen' in order to give the prayer a more suitable ending for use in public worship. But both beginning and ending of the prayer are significant and deliberate. To declare that God is our Father is to turn our back on the devil and all his works; more than that, it is to declare war on the devil and all the evil he has wrought in the world, to commit ourselves to bring in the kingdom of God and shatter the gates of hell. The final phrase of the Lord's Prayer is a ringing call to finish the task of driving out the 'prince of this world' (John 12:31). It is tragic that for so many, through the mistranslation 'Deliver us from evil', it has become nothing more than a request to God to give us a trouble-free life.

So the Lord's Prayer isn't something we can comfortably mumble through, smug in the knowledge that God is our Father, there's food in the cupboard, our sins are forgiven, and we have special protection against temptation and difficulties. Rather, to pray it is a life-changing experience, with every potential to change the world.

How should we pray the Lord's Prayer? Every way we can. The Early Church clearly didn't feel that its form was to be set in concrete; Luke gives us a different version from Matthew's and the early Christians happily added the doxology. So we certainly don't have to stick to one form or one way of praying it. We can take our time over the phrases, meditating on them, or applying them in different contexts. In asking for daily bread, for instance, we can start with a personal request for the material necessities of life, then move on to the Bread of life, then broaden our concern to prayer for those around us and the hungry of the world, who need both material and spiritual bread. We can make the Lord's Prayer very personal, or we can set it firmly in our church community, or broaden it to a vision for the coming of the kingdom of God to the ends of the earth. You can pray it right through in less than thirty seconds, or you can spend hours on one phrase or one word, not least the opening *Abba*. I've even found it helpful to take it backwards, starting with deliverance from the devil and ending with the glorious climax of the kingdom, the Name, and the Father.

The key thing, of course, is to keep this familiar old prayer as fresh and dynamic and thrilling as it would have been that first time Jesus told His disciples to pray it. Thus we ensure that it remains a life-changing and world-changing prayer and never lapses back into a monotonous mantra.

Discussion Starters

1. What experiences have you had of the Lord's Prayer being used helpfully and unhelpfully?

    _____

    _____

    _____

    _____

2. Summarise the insights we gained into *Abba*, 'Father' in our earlier study, and then reflect on the two things Jesus adds immediately to it: 'Our' and heavenly ('in heaven') (Matt. 6:9).

    _____

    _____

    _____

    _____

3. Spend time unpacking the meaning and implications of the three great requests: 'Hallowed be your name, your kingdom come, your will be done on earth as it is in heaven' (Matt. 6:9–10). Try setting them in different contexts, eg your own personal life, your local community and the whole world.

    _____

    _____

    _____

    _____

4. How can we make the request 'Give us today our daily bread' (v.11) meaningful and effective, even when our cupboards and freezers are full to overflowing?

    _____

    _____

    _____

    _____

5. 'Forgiveness is the heart of the gospel.' How is this expressed by verses 12 and 14–15?

_____

_____

_____

_____

6. In the light of James 1:13 a better rendering of the first part of verse 13 is 'Do not put us to the test', which is in fact an accurate translation of the Greek word _peirasmos_. Try using 1 Corinthians 10:13, where the word used is again _peirasmos_, to unpack the meaning of this request.

_____

_____

_____

_____

7. How can the story of Job or the story of the crucifixion illustrate for us the difference between 'deliver us from evil' and 'deliver us from the evil one' (v.13)?

_____

_____

_____

_____

Personal Application

There are many ways we can use the Lord's Prayer and its insights to enrich our personal praying. Over the next few days try using a different approach each day. For example, one day you could apply the prayer in the context of your home and family, and on other days in other contexts. At other times you could take just one request from the prayer and use it as a basis for meditative prayer, perhaps in your personal situation, or in some other context.

The Lord's Prayer is full of riches. Explore them, enjoy them, apply them.

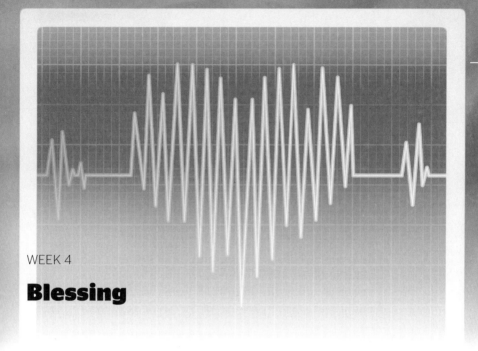

WEEK 4

Blessing

Opening Icebreaker

Ask people to recall various examples of saying 'grace' before (or after) meals, serious and otherwise, that they have come across.

Bible Readings

- Genesis 12:2–3
- Numbers 6:22–27
- Matthew 26:26–29
- Mark 10:13–16
- Luke 9:12–17
- Luke 24:50–52

Focus

We explore the concept of 'blessing' as we look at the prayers of blessing Jesus spoke during His earthly ministry.

Opening Our Eyes

Right at the start of the Bible, against the backdrop of human sin and rebellion against God, God calls Abram and gives him an amazing promise:

> I will make you into a great nation
> and I will bless you …
> and all peoples on earth
> will be blessed through you.' (Gen. 12:2–3)

In this passage, says Paul, God 'announced the gospel in advance'; what's more, he adds, that promise has now been fulfilled; 'the blessing given to Abraham' has 'come to the Gentiles through Christ Jesus, so that by faith we might receive the promise of the Spirit' (Gal. 3:8–9,14).

The blessing that is ours through Christ takes many forms. In this study we're going to focus on one simple way it was expressed, following through those prayers of Jesus where He spoke a blessing. Though differing translations are used, the Greek word used in these accounts means literally 'speak well'; it gives us a picture of Jesus speaking the creative empowering enriching word of God into a person's life or situation. As we know from Isaiah 55:10–11 such a word is always effective.

Among the blessings Jesus pronounced was the blessing on food at a meal, such as on the loaves and fish at the feeding of the 5,000, on the bread at the Last Supper, and on the meal at Emmaus (Mark 6:41; Matt. 26:26; Luke 24:30). In each case the NIV has changed the word 'bless' to 'give thanks', although it keeps 'bless' in other places such as the blessing of the children and of the disciples (Mark 10:16; Luke 24:50–51). Though the concept of 'giving thanks' is undoubtedly present in the blessing over a meal, what Jesus was doing was more than just saying 'Thank You', and we will keep the meaning 'bless' when looking at these passages, while accepting that the element of thanksgiving is also important.

One of the ways I find most helpful to understand a biblical concept is to understand it first as it relates to God, and only then to look at it in the context of our world or our lives. Thus, if I want to know what truth or love really is I don't start with philosopher's truth or mother's love; I examine them first as they are in God, and only then try to fit them into my experience or the world around me. So, instead of analysing blessing as, say, part of our personal experience, we need to start with God and ask: 'What does it mean that God is the Blessed One? What is the blessedness that He has and that He wants to pass on to us as He speaks words of blessing?' In that context we can note that the greatest of all Old Testament blessings (the one God commanded the priests to say over the people) makes it clear that the essence of blessing is nothing less than God Himself, the LORD, summed up in all the wonder of His name:

> "'The LORD bless you
> and keep you;
> the LORD make his face shine upon you
> and be gracious to you;
> the LORD turn his face towards you
> and give you peace."

'So they will put my name on the Israelites, and I will bless them.' (Num. 6:24–27)

Discussion Starters

1. Mark 10:13–16. Matthew unpacks the request in verse 13 for Jesus to 'touch' the children with the words 'for him to place his hands on them and pray for them' (Matt. 19:13). How might this help our understanding of the act of 'blessing'? What do you think is the special significance of 'touch' or the placing or laying on of hands? What difference do you think it made to the children that they had been 'blessed' by Jesus?

_____
_____
_____
_____

2. As far as we can see, Jesus prayed a blessing over every meal. Despite the NIV translation (see previous page) this was more than just giving thanks; it was asking for God's blessing on the food, on the act of eating together, and thus on all who were present. The practice of 'saying grace', even in Christian families, seems to be on the decline. What is the point of continuing (or restoring) the practice? What might we do to make it more significant?

_____
_____
_____
_____

3. Matthew 26:26–29. What is the special 'blessing' in sharing in bread and wine as Jesus has commanded us?

_____
_____
_____
_____

4. Luke 24:50–52. What is the significance of Jesus lifting up His hands (v.50; see a parallel incident in Exod. 17:10–13)? What 'blessing' do you think Jesus imparted as He left His disciples? What significance might there be in Luke's carefully recorded observation that He was still blessing them as He disappeared into heaven?

_____
_____
_____
_____

5. 'I will not let you go unless you bless me,' said Jacob after a night of struggling with God (Gen. 32:26). And God did bless him, on at least two occasions (Gen. 32:29, 35:9). What does it mean that God in Christ pronounces His blessing over us today?

_____
_____
_____
_____

Personal Application

Read Numbers 6:22–27. It is significant that the primary initiative for the blessing of God's people in the Bible comes from God and not from the people. It seems that He is more ready to bless than we are to seek His blessing. This is illustrated in the command God gave the Old Testament priests to speak God's blessing again and again over the people (v.23) and His firm commitment to bless them (v.27).

Find time to meditate on this great blessing (vv.24–26), receiving afresh the many riches God is offering here.

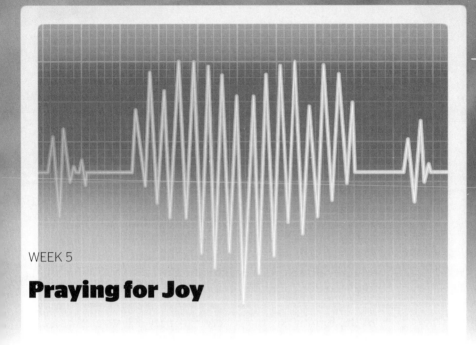

WEEK 5

Praying for Joy

Opening Icebreaker

Invite members of the group, if they can, to recite a
prayer by heart; perhaps one they learnt as a child, one
that has a special significance for them or one they've
learnt through hearing it many times.

Bible Reading

• John 17

Focus

We pick out some of the major themes of this great
prayer, especially aware that Jesus' concern in praying it
was that we should have the full measure of His joy.

Opening Our Eyes

I sometimes have a problem with people who seem to use their public prayers to pass on information to their listeners, or even to preach mini sermons at them. We're supposed to be talking to God, I feel, not to each other. But I mustn't be too quick to judge, since Jesus was clearly conscious of His listening disciples as He prayed this great prayer, and He put in plenty to teach and encourage them. Indeed, in verse 13 He clearly states why He's saying what He's saying: 'so that they may have the full measure of my joy within them.' So here's a prayer designed, among other things, to fill us to overflowing with divine joy. As we study it today, let's make that the key to unlock some of its treasures.

In the form it is written here this prayer lasts about two minutes. Almost certainly the actual prayer Jesus prayed was much longer, just as the discourse in the Upper Room (John 14–16) would have been a lot longer than the nine or ten minutes John's summary would take. John, through the Holy Spirit, has recorded for us the main themes of the prayer, probably including a number of telling phrases that stuck in his mind or in the minds of those who were there.

Amazingly, so short a time before Gethsemane and all the darkness that followed, the word that is most on Jesus' lips in this prayer is 'glory'; we find 'glory' or 'glorify' a total of nine times. This glory is the eternal glory of the triune God, expressed specifically in the life, death, resurrection, ascension and eternal reign of Jesus (vv.1,4–5,24) but wonderfully also given to and expressed in His followers (verses 22 and 10). A glorious source of joy!

Another central theme of this prayer, and another great source of our joy, is our relationship with the Father. Jesus picks this up in verses 2–3,6–8,20–23,26. Christ's supreme work has been to make it possible for us to know Him and share in His eternal life.

A third element of the prayer is the mission of His people. They are being sent into the world, into alien territory (vv.14,16), to continue the mission that Jesus has begun (v.18); they go with the 'words' Jesus has given them from His Father (vv.8,14), the word that is 'truth' (v.17), the 'message' that will bring others to Jesus (v.20) and enable 'the world' to believe in Him (vv.21,23). For this mission to succeed in a hostile world dominated by 'the evil one' two things are essential: divine protection (vv.11–12,15) and oneness with God and with one another (vv.11,21–23).

We'll be picking up in our study these three elements of glory, our relationship with the Father, and our mission. As you work through this great prayer, try to keep two things in mind. First, when Jesus prayed it He was praying specifically for you (v.20), so you can receive the truths of this chapter as very personal for you. Then, as we've seen, Jesus' desire through this study is that you may have in you 'the full measure of [his] joy' (v.13).

Discussion Starters

1. 'Glory' and 'glorify' (John 17:1,4–5,10,22,24) are common enough words in the Bible and in our songs of worship. What do they mean? Why did Jesus say 'the time has come' (v.1) for the Son and the Father to be glorified?

    _____
    _____
    _____
    _____

2. Verses 9–10. What did Jesus mean by 'glory has come to me through them'? What implications has that for us today?

    _____
    _____
    _____
    _____

3. Verses 22–23. Not only do we give glory to God; He gives it to us. What does this mean? In what ways is it expressed?

    _____
    _____
    _____
    _____

4. There are many ways of describing what a Christian is. Looking through verses 2–3,6–8,20–23 and 26, I counted nearly a dozen. Try picking out the ones that strike you most, and rejoice in the knowledge that this is how Jesus sees you.

    _____
    _____
    _____
    _____

5. The word 'sent' comes seven times in this prayer; six times it refers to the mission of Jesus, sent by the Father into the world to bring eternal life. But in verse 18 Jesus transfers His mission to His followers, something He repeats, along with the anointing of the Holy Spirit, in John 20:21–22. What does it mean to be 'sent'? Have we lost the awareness of being 'sent' in this way? If so, how can we regain it?

_____

_____

_____

_____

6. Jesus talks about us having the full measure of His joy in the context of an alien world hating us and the devil attacking us (vv.13–16; see also verses 11–12). How do we make sense of that?

_____

_____

_____

_____

7. What is the oneness Jesus is praying for in verses 11 and 21–23? Why is it so important? What should we be doing about divisions among God's people today?

_____

_____

_____

_____

Personal Application

Is what Jesus is talking about in this great prayer central to my own daily experience? After all, He was praying this prayer for me. Or has my Christian life become dull and routine, or so full of other things that there's no room for what Jesus seems to feel is so important?

Are there things I should list below as a sign that I am committed to giving them the central place in my life that Jesus wants for them?

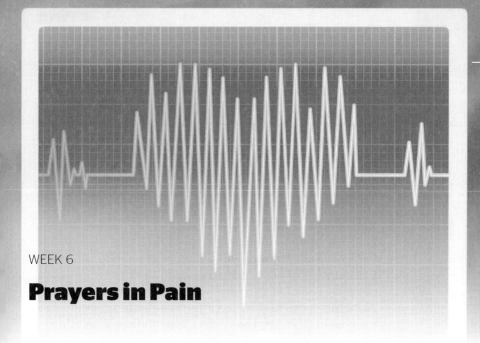

WEEK 6

Prayers in Pain

Opening Icebreaker

Suggest that different members of the group draw a sketch of a Bible character or characters in a very tight spot and the others have to guess who they are.

Bible Readings

- Mark 15:33–36
- Luke 22:39–46
- Luke 23:32–34
- Luke 23:44–47

Focus

We go again to Gethsemane and Calvary and learn from our Saviour as He shows us what it is to pray in pain.

Opening Our Eyes

A few months ago I was taken seriously ill with a mystery disease a thousand miles from home. For the best part of a week the doctors in the intensive care unit struggled to save my life; twice they told Gwen, my wife, that I wasn't going to make it. Those were undoubtedly the darkest days we have ever known. When my daughter who flew out to be with us asked whether I felt the Lord's upholding presence with me I had to answer no. All through those dark days I knew in my mind that the Lord hadn't abandoned me, but the darkness was so complete that I had no sense of Him being with me. Try as I might, I could not experience His presence in prayer.

Early this morning I walked through the fields at the back of our house. The hedges were bursting with May blossom, the woods were glorious with bluebells, the trees were alive with birdsong. It was all so wonderful that I sang aloud the praises of so great a God.

Pain and suffering can never in any way separate us from our Lord Jesus Christ and His love (Rom. 8:35–39), but when the darkness closes in, prayer so often becomes much harder. We've already been reminded that during His earthly life Jesus 'offered up prayers and petitions with loud cries and tears' (Heb. 5:7). In this study we're going to watch Jesus as He goes through the darkness of Gethsemane and the cross; as we listen to four of His prayers in pain we will meet with depths of truth we might never plumb if all our life were a glorious May morning.

It is important to remember that, horrific though the physical sufferings of Jesus in Gethsemane and on the cross may have been, they were tiny compared with His spiritual sufferings. The holy Lamb of God bore the sin of the world; the beloved Son became a curse and tasted

Godforsakenness; the third Person of the triune God was
made sin. It was this, not just the fearsome scourging
and the nails, that Jesus shrank from in Gethsemane; it
was this He was carrying in the darkness of that Friday
afternoon.

In all the agony and darkness of spirit which He suffered
Jesus prayed – and He prayed in an amazing way. Five
times the Gospel writers tell us that the second and third
prayers Jesus prayed on the cross were prayed 'in a loud
voice'. The significance of this may not be immediately
obvious to those of us who have never watched a
crucifixion. Those who have done so know that the
pattern is always the same; the victims grow progressively
weaker and weaker as they fight for breath and life ebbs
from their bodies. Any speech takes an effort; towards the
end the best the victim could utter would be a croak or
a groan. Yet, and Matthew, Mark and Luke all emphasise
this, it was with 'a loud voice' that Jesus shouted His
last prayers, something so amazing that it convinced the
hardened Roman centurion on duty that 'this man was the
Son of God' (Matt. 27:50,54; Mark 15:37,39; Luke 23:46–47).

Discussion Starters

1. Matthew (Matt. 26:36–46) gives us a fuller account of Christ's prayers in Gethsemane; Luke alone adds the details of supernatural strengthening and sweat like drops of blood (Luke 22:39–46). But each Gospel writer makes it abundantly clear that from start to finish Jesus was totally committed to doing His Father's will. Spend time reflecting on that amazing prayer: '… not my will, but yours be done' (Luke 22:42).

   _____
   _____
   _____
   _____

2. Briefly share experiences of when it's been desperately hard to pray '… not my will, but yours be done', or when God has given you the grace to pray them in the most difficult of circumstances. How might you encourage someone who is finding it a real battle to make this his or her prayer?

   _____
   _____
   _____
   _____

3. For many struggling with pain, the prayer 'Father, forgive them …' (Luke 23:34) can be even harder to pray than '… not my will, but yours be done', particularly when the pain is being caused by the one they're called on to forgive. But this prayer of Jesus as He is nailed to the cross is the model we're called to follow (Matt. 6:12,14–15). For reflection: Do we have to wait for a person to repent or apologise before we pray for God to forgive him/her? Can we ask God to forgive others if we ourselves are unwilling to forgive them? What if the offer of forgiveness is refused? When we pray for forgiveness for those who cause us pain,

what difference does our prayer make to us?

_____

_____

_____

_____

4. Picture Mark 15:33–34: whatever was happening in
the darkness of the cross was for each of us and our
salvation. This is the first of the two prayers Jesus
cried out just before dying. No gasping whimper, but
a strong, loud cry of appalling horror and unshakeable
trust. Jesus consciously quotes Psalm 22, which speaks
so vividly of His suffering upon the cross, and yet is
shot through with trust and hope in the One whom He
could still call 'My God'. Is it wrong for us to cry out
'Why?' in our pain? When others cry 'Why?' how might
we respond? How might we help a Christian friend who
feels that she or he has been utterly forsaken by God?

_____

_____

_____

_____

5. 'Our people die well,' said John Wesley of the early
Methodists. Contrary to what always happened with
victims of crucifixion Jesus died with a shout
(Luke 23:46). His confident words were perhaps
another conscious quotation from a great psalm of
trust (Psa. 31:5), prefixed once again with His special
Abba. Could you share any experience of watching
a Christian 'die well' with the group? In contrast to
previous generations we seem reticent these days to
think or talk about dying; why do you think this is so?
How might we prepare ourselves to 'die well'?

_____

_____

_____

_____

Personal Application

I guess you, like me, have been amazed and humbled
by each of these four amazing prayers. Even in the midst
of the most terrible darkness Jesus remained totally
committed to the will of His Father. He overflowed with
love and mercy and grace even to those who tortured
and killed Him; 'Godforsaken' and confronted with death,
He continued wholly trusting with triumphant confidence
in His Father God. Perhaps your response has been one
of shame that you fall so far behind the example of your
Lord in one or more of these areas. If so, be encouraged.
We all fall short, and being aware of our failure is the
first step towards doing something about it. Seek His
forgiveness; study further His example and the teaching of
His Word; open your heart and mind to the transforming
power of the Holy Spirit; pray that He will give you 'the
mind of Christ' so that, however great the darkness and
pain you are called to suffer, His light will shine in you
and through you for His glory.

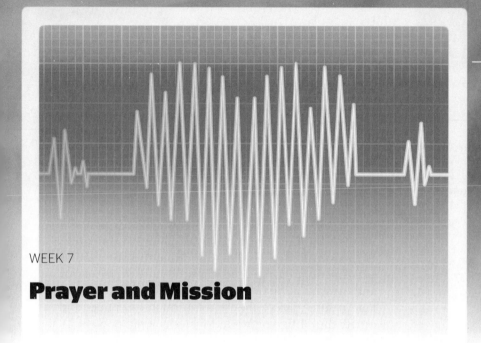

WEEK 7

Prayer and Mission

Opening Icebreaker

Write out (or ask the members of the group to write out and bring) a few highly complex statements and then ask the group to reduce them to something a child could understand (eg 'Woody perennial organisms of the rosaceous genus project visible radiation in the approximate wavelength range 740–620 nanometres' = 'Roses are red').

Bible Readings

- Luke 10:21–24
- Romans 8:31–34
- Hebrews 7:23–25
- 1 John 2:1–2

Focus

As we study the prayer Jesus prayed in His joy when the seventy-two returned and reported great blessing in their mission, we will pick up His themes of revelation and provision and relate them to our own response to His call to mission.

Opening Our Eyes

Picture the scene: seventy-two very ordinary people sent out by Jesus to proclaim the glories and mysteries of the kingdom of God, and to bring the presence of that kingdom into people's lives. Picture them fearful and hesitant at first, 'like lambs among wolves', aware that in some places they'll get a rough reception, and in others they'll be confronted with demonic powers. But then picture them coming back overflowing with joy at what they'd experienced (Luke 10:1–20). Then bring it up to date: the twenty (or the hundred or whatever) very ordinary people that make up your church or group being sent out by the same Jesus with the same task and the same power and resources ...

Little wonder that Jesus is thrilled at the report of the seventy-two and bursts out with joy and praise (Luke 10:21). We can guess that He finds in their successful mission a foretaste of the ultimate fulfilment of God's great purpose of grace, that of bringing men and women, and the whole of creation, back into a living relationship with Himself. He marvels at the way that purpose is working out: how it starts in the heart of the Father, and moves through the Son not to 'the wise and learned' but to 'little children'. Now, He tells His disciples, they are seeing the beginnings of the fulfilment of what prophets and kings have longed to see, the coming of God's great kingdom (vv.23–24).

It is worth noting that the heart of the prayer of Jesus in Luke 10:21–22 is praise and worship at the profound truths of the purposes of God: 'the mystery of his will according to his good pleasure, which he purposed in Christ', as Paul put it in Ephesians 1:9. Though we can be confident that God always hears even the simplest of prayers, there should also be a place in our praying for wonder and worship at the deep mysteries of His being and His ways.

Matthew follows his account of the prayer with Jesus' lovely invitation, 'Come to me, all you who are weary and burdened, and I will give you rest. Take my yoke upon you and learn from me, for I am gentle and humble in heart, and you will find rest for your souls. For my yoke is easy and my burden is light' (Matt. 11:28–30). It is in Jesus Himself that people will find all that the Father offers. It is the cry of Jesus that all will come to Him.

In today's study we are going to keep the context of our own mission very much in our minds as we let this prayer of Jesus remind us of two essential elements of God's mission to the world through Christ, namely revelation and provision. Then we're going to add to these two an element touched on by John, Paul and the writer to the Hebrews. This is Jesus' continuing intercession or advocacy for us before the Father, now that He is at the right hand of God. Though this may be a form of prayer different from His praying while on earth, it is one which provides a powerful basis for our continuing relationship with the Father and our continuing effectiveness in the mission to which He has called us.

Discussion Starters

1. Luke 10:21–22: 'Joy', 'praise' and some profound truths. Are there things we might learn from these three aspects of this prayer that could enrich our own praying?

_____

_____

_____

_____

2. Five times in this short prayer Jesus refers to God as 'Father'. But He also, unusually, adds 'Lord of heaven and earth'. What do you think is the special significance of this?

_____

_____

_____

_____

3. Central to the prayer is the theme of the revelation of God's truth, and especially the truth of God's kingdom come in Christ. These are truths God wants everyone to know (Luke 10:1–2; 1 Tim. 2:3–4). What can we learn from this prayer that will help us play our part in the bringing of that revelation to those around us?

_____

_____

_____

_____

4. Another key theme is provision. In verse 22 Jesus states that the Father has committed all things to Him; so in Jesus we have all the riches of the Father, as Paul triumphantly states (Rom. 8:32). Try listing the problems and difficulties we encounter in our mission and then see how God in Christ has provided for them among the 'all things'.

_____
_____
_____
_____

5. Romans 8:31–34; Hebrews 7:23–25; 1 John 2:1–2. These verses assure us that Jesus hasn't left us to get on with the task of mission on our own; He's there in heaven backing us, particularly when we feel condemned (Rom. 8:34), insecure (Heb. 7:25), or a failure (1 John 2:1). Spend a few minutes drawing encouragement from these verses. How do they relate to Jesus' promise that, as we go, He is with us always (Matt. 28:19–20)?

_____
_____
_____
_____

6. As we conclude our studies of the prayers of Jesus, share with other members of your group how these studies have helped or challenged you in your own praying.

_____
_____
_____
_____

Personal Application

Granted you're not one of the Twelve, how would you feel about being one of the seventy-two? Have another look at Luke 10:1–20; can you not accept this as Jesus' call to you? Think of the joy it would bring to His heart if you could come with joy and say the words of verse 17 to Him. Think too of the joy it would bring to your heart if you could hear Him say those wonderful words of verses 18 to 20 and 23 to 24 directly to you.

Why not use the space below to record any specific things the Spirit of God has been saying to you in this study, or in any of the studies, and add your personal response?

Leader's Notes

Week 1: *Abba*

Discussion Starters

1. It is important to keep in mind that there are many different ways of addressing God in the Bible, and that all of them have a place. In particular, what may be appropriate in one context may be inappropriate in another (see Discussion Starter 5). The aim, however, of this study is to challenge the group to consider whether we might be missing something of the wonder of prayer by our comparative neglect of the riches that underlie the use of *Abba*.

2. The aim here is to try to build up a picture of God as Father, starting with concepts that are at least partly familiar to us. But (as Paul seems to hint in Ephesians 3:14–15) since ultimate fatherhood is primary in God and only derivative in human fathers, using our limited experiences may be sadly inadequate. It would be quite justifiable for the group to use biblical revelation (for example, the story of the prodigal son) to picture the nature of God's fatherhood. It may be that someone in the group raises at this point the issue of a really bad experience of their human father, and you may feel it wise to go straight to Discussion Starter 6. But try to avoid being too distracted from the focus on God as *Abba*.

3. You might point out that the earliest use of Thou/Thee was actually as the intimate singular form in English, like *Du* in German or *tu* in French. There's been something of a tendency among preachers to stress the 'baby talk' element of *Abba* at the expense of the image of the mature adult addressing his or her father in terms of closest intimacy coupled with appropriate respect. Try

to ensure that discussion on this topic doesn't polarise issues. It is not a case of either intimacy or reverence, either a God we love or we fear. Instead it's a matter of each element enriching the other. Try to get the group to picture how we can combine the different elements in our approach to God, and how each can make the other more meaningful.

4. The emphasis here should be on 'drawing near' and 'our heavenly Father'. Our interest is not, say, in the theology of prayer or what we should be asking for; rather it is to discover how we might have in prayer that beautiful relationship with God that Jesus expressed in *Abba*. So try to keep the discussion focused on this aspect. To overcome reticence it may be best for you as leader to start by describing your own experience and approach. It might also help to feed in a few questions, such as, 'Does anyone use meditation? Can you give those of us who've never done it some hints on how to start?'; 'What about words and sentences – do we always have to articulate our personal prayers?'; 'Has anyone found the use of imagination or devotional hymns or poetry helpful?' Along with Discussion Starters 2 and 7, this discussion point is the core of this Bible Study: encouraging each member of the group to have the relationship with God in prayer that Jesus promised us in *Abba*.

5. Besides re-emphasising the wide variety in types of prayer and approaches to prayer, this Discussion Starter can serve to dispel the common assumption that we must model all our praying on the sort of prayers we hear in church.

6. This is, of course, a major issue for many, and you may well be aware that it is a live issue for one or more members of your group. In that case you will need to use your discretion as to how and when to introduce this Discussion Starter, and how much time to spend on it. Do be careful, however, to ensure that the focus of the study

remains on the glories of *Abba* and is not hijacked by bad experiences of fatherhood.

7. Make sure you leave time for this one!

Week 2: Prayers Jesus Didn't Pray

The aim of today's study is to help the members of the group move forward towards maturity in their understanding and practice of prayer. By watching Jesus at prayer, and, in particular, reflecting on occasions when He refrained from a specific prayer, we can move on from a simplistic concept of prayer as an easy way of getting what we want to something nearer what it was for Jesus.

The members of your group will, of course, be at different points in their growth towards maturity in prayer, and some may well still be at the beginning of the process. It will be important at some stage to point out that it is not necessarily wrong to pray childish or self-centred prayers; there will be times when such prayers are appropriate and, even when they are not particularly appropriate, God still hears them and may well choose to answer them. But the thrust of the study will be that praying that stays at this level is very limited and unworthy of a mature follower of the Lord Jesus.

In the passages to be studied Jesus chooses not to do three things:

1. To pray for an easy way out for Himself when faced with a horrific situation (Matt. 26:53; John 12:27).

2. To pray for an easy way out for Peter when he was faced with Satanic onslaught and personal disaster (Luke 22:31–32).

3. To do all the praying for His followers so that they don't have to do any (John 16:26).

As a background to these passages we have the passage in Hebrews 5:7–10 which seems to shame our easy praying, and introduces us to levels of prayer that most of us know little about.

Discussion Starters
1. The main point to bring out here is that a prayer for an easy way out of a difficult situation may not be God's best plan for us. Of course, God has the right, when we do pray for the easy way out, to respond No. But better still for us to face the fact God may have some purpose to be fulfilled through our suffering and take that into consideration in our praying. A secondary point, but still very important, is that all our praying should be in accordance with Bible teaching (v.54). If there's time you might like to use James 1:2–4 as an application of this point.

2. and 3. Besides re-emphasising that we should not necessarily pray to be taken out of a difficult situation, this passage gives us another criterion by which to test our praying, in addition to accordance with Bible teaching: we should pray for what will glorify our Father's name. It may be helpful to stress the contrasting pronoun/adjective in the two prayers: 'Save *me* from this hour', 'Glorify *your* name'.

4. Any answer to the question 'Why do you think Jesus didn't pray for an easy time for Peter?' must necessarily be speculative, but it can be useful to consider how Jesus might have been preparing Peter for future ministry through this experience. If you have time you might invite the members of the group to recount parallel experiences of their own where they can now understand the reason why God allowed them to go through some really tough time.

5. John 16:26 is a verse that has puzzled many and could be open to several interpretations. It forms, of course, something of a climax to the whole Upper Room discourse (John 14–16). Jesus is preparing His disciples for the new situation in which He will no longer be with them in the relationship they have known for the past three years, but in a new relationship through the indwelling Holy Spirit. We can understand Jesus as saying, 'Up to now I've been here to do everything for you, including leading in prayer. But that time's coming to an end; from now on it is over to you; I'm sending you into the world (John 17:18) to serve and to suffer, enabled and empowered by the Holy Spirit. Instead of being spoon fed, you will be witnesses and martyrs; instead of depending on my prayers, you will win prayer battles yourselves.'

6. Again, some members of the group may be willing to share something from their personal experience.

7. Be careful to avoid making anyone feel guilty for praying prayers like these – we all do it, and there are times when such prayers are fully appropriate. But maybe there are times when they are not.

Week 3: The Lord's Prayer

For the purpose of this study we will use Matthew's version of the Lord's Prayer; Luke's is a slightly abbreviated version, but in all essential points it follows Matthew's. Contemporary research and scholarship is virtually unanimous in making two significant changes to the traditional close of the prayer. The doxology, 'For yours is the kingdom and the power and the glory for ever. Amen', has poor manuscript support and almost certainly was not part of the prayer as Jesus taught it; it was added very early on, probably to provide a more suitable ending for the prayer when it was used in public worship.

The rejection of the translation 'deliver us from evil' in favour of 'deliver us from the evil one' may need a bit more explanation. Both versions are possible translations of the Greek, but two factors make it almost certain that 'the evil one' is correct. Matthew elsewhere (5:37; 13:19,38) uses the same phrase as he uses here to mean the devil, as does the first letter of John no less than five times. Secondly, Greek has two words for 'from'; one (*ek*) tends to be used with things, the other (*apo*) with people; Matthew chooses to use *apo* here. The theological significance of the change in translation is, of course, considerable, as we shall be seeing in Discussion Point 7.

Discussion Starters

1. Don't let the group members spend too long talking about gabbled Lord's Prayers in church services and school assemblies. Use the discussion to point out mistakes to avoid and then go on to share ideas that will enrich our praying.

2. As we saw in our first study, the Aramaic word behind 'Father' is *Abba*. The word order in the original puts 'Father' first, then qualifies it (or, rather, enriches it) with 'our' and 'in heaven'.

3. These three requests are so profound and significant you may well spend all the rest of the session unpacking them. It seems very probable that the phrase 'on earth as it is in heaven' (literally 'as in heaven also on earth') is to be taken with all three, so that each of them is saying 'May earth become heaven'. Don't let the members of the group limit 'Hallowed be your name' to 'What a shame "Jesus" is used as a swear word'. Its meaning is, of course, much wider: 'name' covers all that God is, so the request is 'May the whole world recognise God as the

great and glorious God revealed to us in Jesus and the Bible'. Where appropriate, help the group to apply the requests to different contexts; there may be others besides the three I've suggested that would be helpful for your specific group; for example, in our local church situation, in my family, in my place of work or in our nation.

4. Some facts and suggestions you may find useful: 60,000 die of hunger every day worldwide; 1.3 billion live in 'extreme poverty'; 'Christianity is the most materialistic of religions'; we depend on God for everything; God cares about the smallest details of our lives; manna in the wilderness; Proverbs 30:8–9.

5. We'll be picking up the theme of forgiveness when we look at Jesus' prayers on the cross. Since there is so much other material to study here in the Lord's Prayer you may feel it wise to wait until then to discuss this issue.

6. It may be helpful to point out that the Bible teaches that some prayers will always be answered with a Yes (for example, a heartfelt prayer for forgiveness, since God has promised forgiveness to those who truly ask for it), and some prayers may be answered Yes or No (see, for example, Paul's prayer about his 'thorn' in 2 Cor. 12:7–9). The request 'Do not put us to the test' falls into the second category; God does not guarantee always to spare us 'fiery trials' as we saw with Peter, though He does encourage us to pray that where possible we may be spared them.

7. God allowed both Job and Jesus to suffer horrific 'evil', and, in each case, through the suffering, thwarted the designs of the evil one.

Week 4: Blessing

Most people find it hard to wrap their minds around the concept of 'blessing' and, as a result, often have vague or even strange ideas of what it means for us to be blessed by God. In the case of Israel in the Old Testament, the promise of blessing had a strong material aspect (see, for example, Deuteronomy 28:1–14). However this was not so in the original promise of blessing for 'all peoples on earth' given to Abraham (Gen. 12:3), a promise fulfilled, according to Paul, for us through the promised Holy Spirit (Gal. 3:14). You may find it helpful to encourage the group to think of Christ's blessing less in terms of things He gives us and more in terms of His love, grace and presence with us.

Discussion Starters

1. The laying on of hands in the pronouncing of blessings goes back to Genesis 48:12–20. Touch or the placing of hands was often a significant element in Jesus' healing ministry (for example Mark 1:31,41). It is worth encouraging the group to formulate an answer to the question: 'What difference did it make to them that they had been "blessed" by Jesus?', since this can help clarify the concept of blessing in their minds. You may need to try asking further questions like: 'Did it mean they were healthy and wealthy ever after?' 'Did it mean they had a warm glow?' 'Was it just an empty prayer and nothing actually happened?'

2. The act of eating together in Bible days was looked on much more seriously than in today's society. We might think that the food is the central thing; for them the fellowship or communion was central. So a blessing on a meal was much more than 'Lord, help our digestion'; it was 'Lord, enrich our fellowship; be present among us; bind us together as one.' In particular, the host would take responsibility for the wellbeing of his guests (see, for

example, Psalm 23:5–6), so the blessing, spoken by the host, was a commitment by him to do all he could for all who were present.

3. If possible discourage the group from getting bogged down in debate over sacramental versus non-sacramental views of the Lord's Supper. Individuals may like to testify to what taking the bread and wine has meant to them personally; others may need some help in getting a fresh understanding of a practice that has become something of an empty rite to them.

4. Each of the Synoptic Gospels (and Acts 1) records slightly differing aspects of Christ's final commissioning of His disciples. In unpacking the significance of the blessing recorded in Luke it may be helpful to refer the group to Matthew 28:16–20, and consider what parallels there may be in Luke's act of blessing with the phrases, 'All authority in heaven and on earth has been given to me', and 'go and make disciples', and 'I am with you always'.

5. Time may not allow you to get as far as this 'Discussion Starter'. It is designed to help the group summarise what the concept of blessing might mean for us today. In particular, it can help bring out a distinction between the general blessing that is ours in Christ (see, for example, Ephesians 1:3) which is constant and unchanging, and our specific experience of it, which may well come and go.

Week 5: Praying for Joy

This is a long passage compared with the other prayers we're studying in this series, and it contains a great deal of profound material. I've tried to be selective to a degree, picking out one keynote feature and three specific themes. Even so, there's much more material than the average group can cover adequately in one session, so you may well have to be selective.

Discussion Starters

1. There are several aspects to the concept of glory in Bible teaching; a central element running through this chapter is that God should be seen and acknowledged in all the wonder of who He is – great, and holy, and loving, and redeeming at infinite cost. It is in the cross and resurrection that this is seen most clearly; and it is through them that men and women are enabled to have 'eternal life' and 'know' the Father and the Son (vv.2–3). Because of them, not just the redeemed but also all the heavenly powers wonder and adore so great a God.

2. The tense of the verb is past, although some interpreters shy away from the idea that glory had already been brought to Jesus by the lives of His followers, immature and volatile as they were. You might like to refer to Ephesians 3:21.

3. In keeping with the overall purpose of Jesus' prayer, the fullness of joy, try to help the group to get spiritually excited (or to experience glory) about the things Jesus has given us, such as eternal life, knowledge of God, revelation, truth, oneness with God and with each other. And then, of course, there's the final culmination of it all to look forward to (v.24).

4. You could invite each member of the group to choose one, and then unpack it in a few sentences, if possible explaining why it is a source of joy.

5. Jesus also picks up the theme of our being sent in the great commissioning at the end of the other three Gospels (Matthew 28:18–20; Mark 16:15–18; and Luke 24:45–49). See also Acts 1:8.

6. Possible cross references could include Matthew 5:10–12; Acts 5:40–41; Romans 5:3–5; 2 Corinthians 4:15–18; 12:10; James 1:2–4; 1 Peter 4:12–16.

7. Sadly, discussions about the unity Jesus prays for in this chapter can sometimes themselves end up furthering divisions as we express disagreement over ecclesiological and other issues. Do your best to keep the discussion gracious and positive, preferably emphasising what we as individuals could be doing rather than what denominational leaders or those in the other camp should be doing.

Week 6: Prayers in Pain

These four prayers of Jesus take us onto very holy ground; it may be appropriate as the study progresses simply to stop and spend time in awed worship, thanksgiving and response for what Jesus has borne and done for us. Equally, as the Bible passages are read, you may choose to suggest a few moments of silent reflection on each part of the story before you move on to discuss the questions. In keeping with the general pattern of these studies, in which we are seeking to learn things that will enrich our own praying in the light of Jesus' prayers, the Discussion Starters tend to direct attention on us and our praying; but don't let that prevent the group experiencing afresh the wonder of what Jesus did for each one of us on the cross.

Discussion Starters
1 and 2. Be particularly sensitive to the needs of individuals as the group tackles these discussion points. There may well be someone in the group who is still struggling to come to terms with, say, a tragic bereavement. Don't allow the others to pile guilt on them

because as yet they can't really pray this prayer over their experience. You may find it helpful to use the story of the father in Mark 9:24, adapting his cry: 'I do believe; help me overcome my unbelief!'

3. As previously, watch for anyone in the group for whom forgiveness is a particularly difficult issue and, where appropriate, allow that it is OK to say: 'Lord, I do forgive, help me overcome my unforgiveness.'

4. There is profound mystery in this prayer. Be sure to allow the group to worship and wonder as One who is God Himself experiences and carries the penalty of sin, the utter darkness of separation from God. The recording of the Aramaic words which Jesus used makes it evident that He was consciously quoting Psalm 22, with its staggering juxtaposition of the utter darkness of Godforsaken suffering and enduring confidence in the One who is 'My God' and can be utterly trusted in every situation. In discussing the issue of 'Why?' you might like to refer to some of the psalmists' cries: Psa. 10:1,13; 42:5,9; 43:2; 44:23–24; 74:1,10–11; 79:10; and 88:14. It may also be helpful to distinguish between various types of 'Why?'; for example, 'Why?' could be a cry of anguish, or a protest, or a genuine seeking after understanding, or a rebuff.

5. Superficially, dying might seem a pretty morbid topic for discussion. Be sure to keep the conversation positive and creative. You could refer to Stephen's reaction to the experience of a horrible death (Acts 7:54–60) and Paul's attitude to dying (Phil. 1:20–26; 2 Tim. 4:6–8).

Week 7: Prayer and Mission

The prayer of Luke 10:21–22 is set firmly in the context of mission; in Matthew's account it even ends with an appeal (Matt. 11:28–29)! So I've tried to keep that context to the fore in this study. Linking the three passages on the high priestly ministry of Jesus with the prayer in Luke 10 may seem slightly artificial, but there is value in reminding ourselves that Jesus' ministry of prayer is (in at least some sense) continuing today, ensuring for us, however weak we may be, all the riches of God's grace.

Discussion Starters

1. If necessary, remind the group that God delights to hear the simplest of prayers as well as the most profound. Equally, there is a place for prayers that focus on ourselves and our needs, as well as prayers that focus on the great truths of God's revelation in Christ. If time permits you could suggest that the group uses one of the prayers of Paul in his letter to Ephesus (Eph. 1:15–23; 3:14–21) to compare its 'theological' content with that of the kind of prayers we're most used to hearing in church and prayer meetings.

2. You might like to point out the parallel between 'Father, Lord of heaven and earth' and the first four words of Matthew's version of the Lord's Prayer (Matt. 6:9).

3. A passage you might choose to refer to is 2 Corinthians 4:1–7. Points to stress are that the primary key to receiving the truth of God is Jesus (Luke 10:22), and a second essential key is humility (Luke 10:21). Jesus almost certainly had the scribes and Pharisees in mind when He spoke of 'the wise and learned'; He is not saying that intelligence and study are necessarily a block to knowing God's truth, but He is making it clear that a childlike, open, trusting attitude of heart and mind is essential for everyone, learned or otherwise (see Mark 10:15). Jesus

may have the seventy-two in mind when He speaks of God revealing His truths to 'little children', or He may have been thinking of those who listened to them (v.16); most likely He was thinking of both. Both we who are sent out with the message (v.1) and those to whom we go need the openness and trust of a child.

4. John 3:35 and Matthew 28:18 provide helpful parallels to 'All things have been committed to me by my Father'. Since we'll be picking up Romans 8:34 under Discussion Starter 5, it could be helpful at this stage to read Romans 8:31–39, and to point out that Paul is confident that the 'all things' of God's provision extend to 'trouble, hardship, persecution' and the like (Rom. 8:35 and 37; see also 28).

5. Theologians differ over how we are to think of the ministry of intercession which Jesus now exercises for us in heaven. It is only specifically mentioned three times (Rom. 8:34; Heb. 7:25; 1 John 2:1), and each time only briefly. Some feel that Jesus' words in John 16:26 mean that He is not now actually praying for us, at any rate not in the way He used to pray for His disciples. Rather, they suggest, His very presence on the right hand of the throne of God, with the wounds of the cross still visible on Him, is a constant reminder to the Father of what He has done for a lost world, and so a continuing 'prayer' for salvation and the riches of the kingdom. One thing we must definitely reject is any suggestion that the Father is in some way reluctant to accept us or do anything for us, and thus that Jesus has somehow to persuade Him by His intercession on our behalf. Our salvation and every blessing that we receive in Christ has its origin in the heart of the Father God (Eph. 1:3); He does not need to be persuaded. For my own part, I don't think it is necessary for us to know exactly how Jesus intercedes for us. It is enough to know that the presence of the crucified and risen Saviour there on the throne of the universe

guarantees both my acceptance with God and all the rich blessings of His love (Rom. 8:31–39).

National Distributors

UK: (and countries not listed below)
CWR, Waverley Abbey House, Waverley Lane, Farnham, Surrey GU9 8EP.
Tel: (01252) 784700 Outside UK (44) 1252 784700 Email: mail@cwr.org.uk

AUSTRALIA: KI Entertainment, Unit 21 317-321 Woodpark Road, Smithfield, New South Wales
2164. Tel: 1 800 850 777 Fax: 02 9604 3699 Email: sales@kientertainment.com.au

CANADA: David C Cook Distribution Canada, PO Box 98, 55 Woodslee Avenue, Paris,
Ontario N3L 3E5. Tel: 1800 263 2664 Email: sandi.swanson@davidccook.ca

GHANA: Challenge Enterprises of Ghana, PO Box 5723, Accra. Tel: (021) 222437/223249
Fax: (021) 226227 Email: ceg@africaonline.com.gh

HONG KONG: Cross Communications Ltd, 1/F, 562A Nathan Road, Kowloon.
Tel: 2780 1188 Fax: 2770 6229 Email: cross@crosshk.com

INDIA: Crystal Communications, 10-3-18/4/1, East Marredpalli, Secunderabad – 500026, Andhra
Pradesh. Tel/Fax: (040) 27737145 Email: crystal_edwj@rediffmail.com

KENYA: Keswick Books and Gifts Ltd, PO Box 10242-00400, Nairobi.
Tel: (254) 20 312639/3870125 Email: keswick@swiftkenya.com

MALAYSIA: Canaanland, No. 25 Jalan PJU 1A/41B, NZX Commercial Centre, Ara Jaya, 47301
Petaling Jaya, Selangor. Tel: (03) 7885 0540/1/2 Fax: (03) 7885 0545 Email: info@canaanland.com.my

Salvation Publishing & Distribution Sdn Bhd, 23 Jalan SS 2/64, 47300 Petaling Jaya, Selangor.
Tel: (03) 78766411/78766797 Fax: (03) 78757066/78756360
Email: info@salvationbookcentre.com

NEW ZEALAND: KI Entertainment, Unit 21 317-321 Woodpark Road, Smithfield,
New South Wales 2164, Australia. Tel: 0 800 850 777 Fax: +612 9604 3699
Email: sales@kientertainment.com.au

NIGERIA: FBFM, Helen Baugh House, 96 St Finbarr's College Road, Akoka, Lagos.
Tel: (01) 7747429/4700218/825775/827264 Email: fbfm_1@yahoo.com

PHILIPPINES: OMF Literature Inc, 776 Boni Avenue, Mandaluyong City.
Tel: (02) 531 2183 Fax: (02) 531 1960 Email: gloadlaon@omflit.com

SINGAPORE: Alby Commercial Enterprises Pte Ltd, 95 Kallang Avenue #04-00, AIS Industrial
Building, 339420. Tel: (65) 629 27238 Fax: (65) 629 27235 Email: marketing@alby.com.sg

SOUTH AFRICA: Struik Christian Books, 80 MacKenzie Street, PO Box 1144, Cape Town 8000.
Tel: (021) 462 4360 Fax: (021) 461 3612 Email: info@struikchristianmedia.co.za

SRI LANKA: Christombu Publications (Pvt) Ltd, Bartleet House, 65 Braybrooke Place, Colombo 2.
Tel: (9411) 2421073/2447665 Email: dhanad@bartleet.com

USA: David C Cook Distribution Canada, PO Box 98, 55 Woodslee Avenue, Paris, Ontario N3L 3E5,
Canada. Tel: 1800 263 2664 Email: sandi.swanson@davidccook.ca

CWR is a Registered Charity - Number 294387
CWR is a Limited Company registered in England - Registration Number 1990308

Courses and seminars

Publishing and new media

Conference facilities

Transforming lives

CWR's vision is to enable people to experience personal transformation through applying God's Word to their lives and relationships.

Our Bible-based training and resources help people around the world to:
• Grow in their walk with God
• Understand and apply Scripture to their lives
• Resource themselves and their church
• Develop pastoral care and counselling skills
• Train for leadership
• Strengthen relationships, marriage and family life and much more.

Our insightful writers provide daily Bible-reading notes and other resources for all ages, and our experienced course designers and presenters have gained an international reputation for excellence and effectiveness.

CWR's Training and Conference Centre in Surrey, England, provides excellent facilities in an idyllic setting – ideal for both learning and spiritual refreshment.

CWR Applying God's Word
to everyday life and relationships

CWR, Waverley Abbey House,
Waverley Lane, Farnham,
Surrey GU9 8EP, UK

Telephone: **+44 (0)1252 784700**
Email: **info@cwr.org.uk**
Website: **www.cwr.org.uk**

Registered Charity No 294387
Company Registration No 1990308

Dramatic new resource

Galatians - Freedom in Christ
by John Houghton

Unpack the sometimes complex arguments of Paul in his letter to the Galatians, understand the logic of salvation by grace alone, through faith alone in Christ alone, and discover the truth that sets us free!

72-page booklet, 148x210mm
ISBN: 978-1-85345-648-0

The bestselling *Cover to Cover* Bible Study Series

1 Corinthians
Restoring harmony
ISBN: 978-1-85345-374-8

2 Corinthians
Growing a Spirit-filled church
ISBN: 978-1-85345-551-3

1 Timothy
Healthy churches –
effective Christians
ISBN: 978-1-85345-291-8

23rd Psalm
The Lord is my shepherd
ISBN: 978-1-85345-449-3

2 Timothy and Titus
Vital Christianity
ISBN: 978-1-85345-338-0

Acts 1-12
Church on the move
ISBN: 978-1-85345-574-2

Acts 13-28
To the ends of the earth
ISBN: 978-1-85345-592-6

Ecclesiastes
Hard questions and
spiritual answers
ISBN: 978-1-85345-371-7

Elijah
A man and his God
ISBN: 978-1-85345-575-9

Ephesians
Claiming your inheritance
ISBN: 978-1-85345-229-1

Esther
For such a time as this
ISBN: 978-1-85345-511-7

Fruit of the Spirit
Growing more like Jesus
ISBN: 978-1-85345-375-5

Galatians
Freedom in Christ
ISBN: 978-1-85345-648-0

Genesis 1-11
Foundations of reality
ISBN: 978-1-85345-404-2

God's Rescue Plan
Finding God's fingerprints
on human history
ISBN: 978-1-85345-294-9

Great Prayers of the Bible
Applying them to our lives today
ISBN: 978-1-85345-253-6

Hebrews
Jesus – simply the best
ISBN: 978-1-85345-337-3

Hosea
The love that never fails
ISBN: 978-1-85345-290-1

Isaiah 1-39
Prophet to the nations
ISBN: 978-1-85345-510-0

Isaiah 40-66
Prophet of restoration
ISBN: 978-1-85345-550-6

James
Faith in action
ISBN: 978-1-85345-293-2

Jeremiah
The passionate prophet
ISBN: 978-1-85345-372-4

John's Gospel
Exploring the seven miraculous signs
ISBN: 978-1-85345-295-6

Joseph
The power of forgiveness and reconciliation
ISBN: 978-1-85345-252-9

Mark
Life as it is meant to be lived
ISBN: 978-1-85345-233-8

Moses
Face to face with God
ISBN: 978-1-85345-336-6

Nehemiah
Principles for life
ISBN: 978-1-85345-335-9

Parables
Communicating God on earth
ISBN: 978-1-85345-340-3

Philemon
From slavery to freedom
ISBN: 978-1-85345-453-0

Philippians
Living for the sake of the gospel
ISBN: 978-1-85345-421-9

Prayers of Jesus
Hearing His heartbeat
ISBN: 978-1-85345-647-3

Proverbs
Living a life of wisdom
ISBN: 978-1-85345-373-1

Revelation 1-3
Christ's call to the Church
ISBN: 978-1-85345-461-5

Revelation 4-22
The Lamb wins! Christ's final victory
ISBN: 978-1-85345-411-0

Rivers of Justice
Responding to God's call to righteousness today
ISBN: 978-1-85345-339-7

Ruth
Loving kindness in action
ISBN: 978-1-85345-231-4

The Covenants
God's promises and their relevance today
ISBN: 978-1-85345-255-0

The Divine Blueprint
God's extraordinary power in ordinary lives
ISBN: 978-1-85345-292-5

The Holy Spirit
Understanding and experiencing Him
ISBN: 978-1-85345-254-3

The Image of God
His attributes and character
ISBN: 978-1-85345-228-4

The Kingdom
Studies from Matthew's Gospel
ISBN: 978-1-85345-251-2

The Letter to the Colossians
In Christ alone
ISBN: 978-1-85345-405-9

The Letter to the Romans
Good news for everyone
ISBN: 978-1-85345-250-5

The Lord's Prayer
Praying Jesus' way
ISBN: 978-1-85345-460-8

The Prodigal Son
Amazing grace
ISBN: 978-1-85345-412-7

The Second Coming
Living in the light of Jesus' return
ISBN: 978-1-85345-422-6

The Sermon on the Mount
Life within the new covenant
ISBN: 978-1-85345-370-0

The Tabernacle
Entering into God's presence
ISBN: 978-1-85345-230-7

The Ten Commandments
Living God's Way
ISBN: 978-1-85345-593-3

The Uniqueness of our Faith
What makes Christianity distinctive?
ISBN: 978-1-85345-232-1

For current prices or to order visit www.cwr.org.uk/store
Available online or from Christian bookshops.

Cover to Cover Every Day

Gain deeper knowledge of the Bible

Each issue of these bimonthly daily Bible-reading notes gives you insightful commentary on a book of the Old and New Testaments with reflections on a psalm each weekend by Philip Greenslade.

Enjoy contributions from two well-known authors every two months, and over a five-year period you will be taken through the entire Bible.

Only £2.85 each (plus p&p)
£15.50 for UK annual subscription (bimonthly, p&p included)
£13.80 for annual email subscription
(available from www.cwr.org.uk/store)

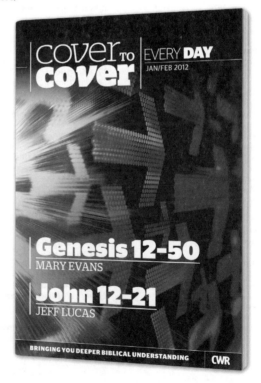

Cover to Cover Complete
Read through the Bible chronologically

Take an exciting, year-long journey through the Bible, following events as they happened.

- See God's strategic plan of redemption unfold across the centuries
- Increase your confidence in the Bible as God's inspired message
- Come to know your heavenly Father in a deeper way

The full text of the flowing Holman Christian Standard Bible (HCSB) provides an exhilarating reading experience and is augmented by our beautiful:

- Illustrations
- Maps
- Charts
- Diagrams
- Timeline

And key Scripture verses and devotional thoughts make each day's reading more meaningful.

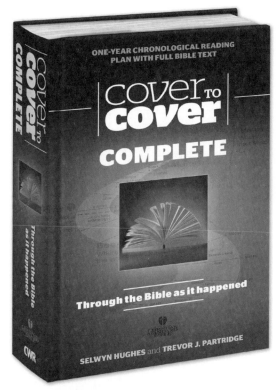

ONE-YEAR CHRONOLOGICAL READING PLAN WITH FULL BIBLE TEXT

cover TO cover COMPLETE

Through the Bible as it happened

SELWYN HUGHES and TREVOR J. PARTRIDGE